If I Was...

– S.D. Bailey –

Illustrations by Trevor Lalaguna

AuthorHouse™
1663 Liberty Drive
Bloomington, IN 47403
www.authorhouse.com
Phone: 833-262-8899

Because of the dynamic nature of the Internet, any web addresses or links contained in this book may have changed since publication and may no longer be valid. The views expressed in this work are solely those of the author and do not necessarily reflect the views of the publisher, and the publisher hereby disclaims any responsibility for them.

Any people depicted in stock imagery provided by Getty Images are models, and such images are being used for illustrative purposes only.
Certain stock imagery © Getty Images.

This book is printed on acid-free paper.

ISBN: 978-1-6655-7412-9 (sc)
ISBN: 978-1-6655-7413-6 (e)

Library of Congress Control Number: 2022919714

Print information available on the last page.

Published by AuthorHouse

Rev. Date: 10/28/2022

authorHOUSE®

Dedications to my wonderful children,
Justice, Kennedy and Mason

If I Was...

If I was a bird, would I fly through the sky?

With all the other birds so very high?

Through the stars, over the clouds, around
the mountains; oh so high I could fly!

Swooping down, high and low, flapping
my wings as hard as they would go.

Chasing my friends, flying through clouds, soaring through the air, putting on quite the show!

If I was a dog... Would I spend my days at play?
Wagging my tail and barking at the neighbors
as if I had something important to say!

Would all the cats and kittens be my friends and stay all day to play? Stay all day just so we could play?

Jumping through the grass, over the fence and
running around the trees as I lead the way?

Oh what fun it would be to play all day until
the sun sets and slowly goes away!

If I was a tree… would my leaves begin to grow?

A great big tree, with branches and leaves, and
even some shade for my sisters ya know.

A tree so big I could stand in the sun, through the rain and even when the strong winds would blow.

I will have my roots deep within the land, wiggling my roots as if my toes were in the sand.

I would be able to use the branches as my hands, stretching out as far as I can!

What *if I was* the sun?

I would play with our dog as he rolls in the grass all day.

Watch him rub on his tummy before
I have to slowly slip away.

I should shine on the trees, the leaves
and make them all grow!

Big trees, little trees, palm trees and
even Christmas trees with a bow!

I could fly with the birds in the sky so
very high. Oh so high I could fly!

Casting my rays through the clouds until the
moon says hi and I must say good-bye.

Yes I could be the sun, making new friends,
hanging around and having some fun.
Oh what fun it is to be the sun!

Making the day bright and all a glow until
the night has come and the day is done.

Trying to catch the moon, chasing it around
the earth all the time second to none.

But what *if I was* the moon?

Printed in the United States
by Baker & Taylor Publisher Services